FACT FILE:
ECHIDNA

By JBus

Library For All Ltd.

Fact File: Echidna

First published 2023

Published by Library For All Ltd
Email: info@libraryforall.org
URL: libraryforall.org

Our Yarning logo design by Jason Lee, Bidjipidji Art

Original illustrations by Kit Turner

Fact File: Echidna
JBus
ISBN: 978-1-923110-42-7
SKU04303

FACT FILE: ECHIDNA

Contents

3

Appearance

Echidnas have short, round bodies, and are covered in spines, also know as quills. These quills are modified hairs that have been enlarged, stiffened, and strengthened.

Spines or quills

Claws

Because of their flexible quills, echidnas can curl into a ball to hide from predators. The quills also protect them while they are in a ball.

Snout

Echidnas can be different shades of brown, and most have white tips on their quills. Some echidnas have longer snouts than others, but they all have powerful claws on their feet. They use these to dig holes to find food or for hiding.

There are four different species of echidna:

Short-beaked echidna

Sir David's long-beaked echidna

Eastern long-beaked echidna

Western long-beaked echidna

8

Eating habits

An echidna's tongue is incredibly long, which is a huge help when eating food. They don't have teeth, so echidnas use their tongues to crush their food against the insides of their mouths. They stick their long tongues into burrows, logs, and mounds to find delicious ants and other insects.

Habitat
Echidnas thrive in their natural habitats or forests and woodland areas. They are native to Australia and exist all across the continent.

Echidnas are solitary animals and they each have their own territories. They shelter in crevices and caves when it's hot and forage at night for food. By burrowing under leaves, they can camouflage themselves from predators.

Predators

Predators are animals that prey on others to survive. The little echidna has a few predators. It needs to look out for hungry dingoes, eagles, foxes, feral cats, and wild dogs. Echidnas will burrow into leaf litter or make holes in the dirt to avoid their predators. Plus, their quills protect them from anything trying to eat them.

Reproduction

Echidnas are mammals. A mammal is a warm-blooded animal that is usually covered in fur and gives birth to live young.

However, the echidna is a different type of mammal called a "monotreme": it lays eggs. The only other Australian monotreme is the platypus.

The females lay one egg at a time and transfer these to a pouch after birth. They incubate the eggs for around 11 days until they hatch. After the young hatch, they travel with their mum in the pouch — much like a kangaroo joey.

Echidnas feed their babies milk through the mammary glands in their pouches.

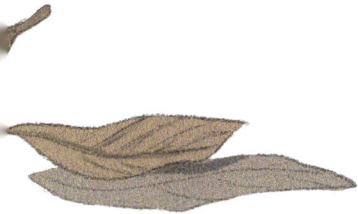

Baby echidnas

Baby Echidnas are called puggles. When they hatch, they have soft, smooth skin and their quills and fur have not grown yet. After several months, the puggle will have the same features as an adult echidna — ready to find their own territory and food.

More Fun Facts
- Echidnas are great swimmers; they look for bodies of water to bathe and groom themselves.
- Echidnas can sense electric currents.
- They can weigh up to six kilograms.
- An echidna's maximum speed is 2.3 kilometres per hour.
- Echidnas can be 33-53 centimetres in length.
- Their average life span in the wild is 10 years, but some live to 16.

Glossary

Word	Meaning
Forage	To wander in search of food
Emerge	To come out of something
Mammal	Warm-blooded animal that births live young
Features	Parts of something
Incubate	Sitting on eggs to keep them warm until they hatch
Habitat	Environment/place that an animal lives
Mammary glands	An organ a female mammal has that produces milk for their young
Predators	Organisms that exist to prey on other organisms
Species	Classes of individuals that have common characteristics or qualities
Camouflage	To hide yourself in the environment around you
Monotreme	A mammal that lays eggs instead of giving live birth

You can use these questions to talk about this book with your family, friends and teachers.

What did you learn from this book?

Describe this book in one word. Funny? Scary? Colourful? Interesting?

How did this book make you feel when you finished reading it?

What was your favourite part of this book?

download our reader app
getlibraryforall.org

About the author

JBus is a Kabi Kabi woman from Queensland and lives in Brisbane. She enjoys being at the beach with her family, creating art and singing.

Author's Country

Darwin

NORTHERN
TERRITORY

QUEENSLAND

WESTERN
AUSTRALIA

SOUTH
AUSTRALIA

Brisb

NEW SOUTH
WALES

Perth

Adelaide

Sydney

ACT
Canberra

VICTORIA
Melbourne

TASMANIA
Hobart

Our Yarning

Want to discover more books from this collection? Our Yarning is a collection of books written by Aboriginal and Torres Strait Islander peoples across Australia.

We know that children learn better, and enjoy reading more, when they see themselves in the stories, characters and illustrations of the books they read.

To download the app, visit the Google Play Store on any Android device and search 'Our Yarning'.